D1526282

TOBACCO DOGS

PERROS DE TABACO

Ana Minga

translated from the Spanish by Alexis Levitin

For Ann,   Nov. 15, 2013

a plaintive dog to
sympathize with Flannery,
from your ever older pal,

BITTER OLEANDER
P R E S S

2013

The Bitter Oleander Press
4983 Tall Oaks Drive
Fayetteville, New York 13066-9776
USA

www.bitteroleander.com
info@bitteroleander.com

ISBN 10: 0-9883525-1-6
ISBN 13: 978-0-9883525-1-3

Library of Congress Control Number: 2013948663

Backcover Photograph of Ana Minga by Guillermo Vicuna

Layout & Design: Roderick Martinez

Cover Painting: *Perro semihundido*. 1820-1823, by Francisco De Goya
        Oil on canvas. Madrid. Prado Museum (source: Art Resource, NY)

Distributed in the United States by Small Press Distribution, Inc.
Berkeley, CA 94710-1409
www.spdbooks.org

Manufactured in the United States of America

ACKNOWLEDGMENTS

I must thank my colleague Fernando Iturburu for introducing me to his homeland, Ecuador, and to many of its finest poets, including Ana Minga. We included her work along with that of seventeen other contemporary Ecuadorian poets in our collaborative effort, *Tapestry of the Sun: An Anthology of Ecuadorian Poetry* (Coimbra Editions, 2009). I am delighted to thank, as well, Ana Minga, who worked with me on these translations both in Guayaquil and in Quito. Much gratitude, as well, to SUNY Plattsburgh for supporting my travel to Ecuador to work on this book. Also thanks to CEN for providing an essential workplace for me in Guayaquil. And thanks to Dromedario, Sagres, Portugal, for giving me extensive use of their computer as the text received its final revisions.

When it comes to the quality of the final translations, I am deeply grateful to three people: my colleague Diana Sarabia Acosta, here at SUNY Plattsburgh, and my two good old friends Elizabeth Andrews and Fred Fornoff. All three of them gave my translation a meticulous reading and helpfully nudged me ever closer to the faithful rendering of the spirit of the original that is every literary translator's true goal. If the reader finds any shortcomings in the English text, the responsibility is entirely my own.

I would like to thank the California Institute of Arts and Letters for publishing *Tapestry of the Sun*, the anthology in which eight of these poems first appeared. Special thanks to Paul B. Roth as well, who dedicated a generous feature to Ana Minga in *The Bitter Oleander* (Vol.16; No. 2). I would also like to thank the editors of the following literary magazines in which many of these poems, sometimes in slightly different versions, made their first appearance:

Asheville Poetry Review
The Bitter Oleander
Blue Lyra
Boulevard
Ezra
Hampden-Sydney Poetry Review
Metamorphoses
Per Contra
Plume
Rosebud

CONTENTS

Cajon de ruidos / Drawer Full of Noise

Pandemonium / Pandemonium

PREFACE

Goya's *Perro Semihundido*, found on the cover of this book, is the most poignant depiction of the human condition I have ever encountered. The universe is reduced to mounting dark earth seemingly on the verge of engulfing a small, half-hidden creature, while the background offers nothing but a curtain of greenish-grey hopelessness. This is not just one small dog. It is each of us waiting to be swallowed by the earth, surrounded by a universe that says nothing.

In a lengthy interview granted me in Quito, in late July of 2009, Ana Minga reflected on her relationship with dogs: "My first, my only, and still my best friends have been dogs. I have written often about dogs. Right now I am working on a book of poems exclusively about dogs. In all sincerity, I prefer dogs to humans." Earlier in the interview, she recalled her childhood growing up in the vast, luxurious Opus Dei establishment where her father worked: "Starting at the age of eleven, I began to suffer from insomnia, but I dealt with the problem by wandering around in the night, enjoying the lovely woods, the rose bushes, the full moon lying on the meadows. My solitary night walks were not entirely solitary: I was accompanied by my five pet dogs....The dogs were my best friends and they went everywhere with me. In fact, they were my only friends in the Opus Dei world...."

As we can see, Ana Minga has appropriated those dogs of her childhood and transformed them into essential characters in many of her poems. She has great compassion for her strays, her street dogs, and clearly identifies with them. After all, it is she and her human friends who ceaselessly smoke, not the literal dogs that share the lonely streets with them. It is clear that the poet feels that she herself is one of them. In the very first *Tobacco Dog* poem, for example, she quickly shifts from the normative third person to the first person: Street dogs don't believe in guardian angels/ the sin of being survivors follows us/with tons of coughing in our throats/ we are faithful unto death." And towards the end of the book, in *Pandemonium* E she says: "Now I understand dogs/ to have a bone stuck in your throat/ is a serious matter."

Ana Minga is always on the side of the beaten, the down-trodden, the marginalized, all beings threatened by dissolution and death, whether mongrel dogs or incarcerated lunatics. Her last published book *Pajaros huérfanos (Orphaned Birds)* is set in an insane asylum, where she spent time doing research as both journalist and poet. Many of those painfully inventive, at times fantasmagoric poems, appeared in *The Bitter Oleander*, Vol. 16, No. 2. But that is another book. For the moment, let us be content with this grim vision, originally titled *Behind God's Back*. Let us think of Hieronymus Bosch. Let us think of Francis Bacon. Let us think of Goya. These, to my mind, are her anguished compatriots.

— Alexis Levitin, June/2013

Estuve aquí.
Me ahogaron contra el muro.

I was here.
They rubbed me out against the wall.

— David Ledesma

TOBACCO DOGS

PERROS DE TABACO

A los perros que he tenido.
To the dogs I have had.

I

Los perros de la calle no creemos en ángeles de la guarda
nos persigue el pecado de ser sobrevivientes
con kilos de tos en la garganta
somos fieles hasta en la muerte.

Mordemos zapatos desconocidos
desde el diente amarillo nos sale hambre.
Algunas veces damos pena
se compadecen
en el mercado nos dan un pellejo
y con un poco de suerte
una mirada
pero nada más
pues les asusta nuestra inocencia.

Sabemos bien quiénes son nuestros castigadores
pero no los mordemos
porque dejaríamos de ser perros buenos
nos convertiríamos en perros con rabia
perfectos terroristas vagamundos
para una eliminación con excusas.

Acudimos al parque
para hallar indicios de nuestra espera en la esquina
una huella de los colegas que solían descansar bajo los árboles
una huella del amigo que cuando aullaba
su pensamiento nos daba la vuelta en los huesos

siempre creímos que nos "aullaba su último minuto"
pues él como nosotros
no conoció abuelos
ni otros parientes
sólo el dolor que balbucea en las botellas de vino.

Aunque somos muchos los perros de la calle
cada cual transita con su horizonte
cada cual tiene su hueso atravesado en la garganta
cada cual muerde el silencio.

I

Street dogs don't believe in guardian angels
the sin of being survivors follows us
with tons of coughing in our throats
we are faithful unto death.

We've been biting unknown shoes
since hunger emerged from our yellow tooth.
Sometimes they feel sorry
and they pity us
in the market they give us scraps
and with a bit of luck
they give a glance
but nothing more
for they are frightened by our innocence.

We know well enough the ones who punish us
but we don't bite them
because if we stop being good dogs
we will become rabid dogs
full-fledged worldwide terrorist vagabonds
perfect for justifiable elimination.

We gather in the park
sniffing for traces of our waiting on the corner
some sign of colleagues who used to rest beneath the trees
or of a friend who when he howled
the thought of him would make its way around our bones

we always thought he had "howled his last " for us
because he like us
knew no grandparents
or other relatives
just the pain that babbles in bottles of wine.

Just the same we street dogs are important
each of us walks with his own horizon
each has his own bone stuck in his throat
each one gnaws his own silence.

Escribimos sobre lo que nos pasa
pues de esa madera estamos hechos.

Buscamos lo que no existe
como humanos buscando señales de Dios
como perros ingenuos
creyendo que en la próxima calle
está el sol.

We write about what happens to us
for that's the stuff we're made of.

We search for what does not exist
like humans seeking signs of God
like ingenuous dogs
who believe that on the next street
the sun is shining.

II

Ay mi pobre diablo
así mismo son
han de sacarte de la guarida
culpa tras culpa ha de caerte
sólo yo sé
que estás en delirio
destruyendo con tu anatomía
olvidos planeados.

Sólo yo sé
de tu interés por los niños
que para nacer se han sujetado de innombrables.
Los persigues
los inquietas
adviertes que vas dibujado por el mundo
con sus mismas vestiduras.

No te interesan las horas por delante
no quieres que ningún tiempo
te cuente los dientes rotos
prefieres acariciar pacientemente cuerpos simétricos
y cuidas a las almas perdidas
pues reconoces que son la más exquisita anestesia.

Sé también que a veces
el cordón umbilical te aprieta el cuello

que te viene una fe viva en la muerte
que lloras como un recién nacido
que te despiertas en la madrugada
sólo
para describir tu infierno.

II

Ay, my poor devil
that's exactly how they are
they have to pull you from your hiding place
guilt upon guilt will be your share
only I know
that you're delirious
destroying with your anatomy
your planned oblivion.

Only I know
of your concern for children
who to be born submit to namelessness.
You follow them
you disturb them
you warn them of your passing through the world like a sketch
in their very own clothes.

You don't care about the hours that lie ahead
you don't want time ever
to count your broken teeth
you prefer to patiently caress symmetric bodies
while looking after lost souls
because you recognize that they're the most exquisite anaesthetic.

I also know that sometimes
the umbilical cord twists round your neck
that a lively faith in death comes over you

that you cry like a newborn child
that you wake up early in the morning
only
to describe your hell.

III

El Rompenucas volvía en la noche
sólo era la vida en un niño destartalado
pero ni pensar en hacer ruido
gritar
pedir auxilio
había que callar
correr a la oscuridad
ver la procesión de fantasmas
escuchar a una madre comer las vísceras de su hijo
sentir a un padre seudo alacrán regar tumores en el cerebro.

Salir al campo
darle un trago al Rompenucas
olerse la tierra en las zanjas de las manos
mirarse la necedad de resistir
para que la soledad no esté tan triste
en la confusión de esta morgue que elimina a los archivos viejos.

III

The *Rompenucas* came back in the night
it was just the life inside a huddled worn-out child
who didn't even think of making a sound
screaming
calling for help
he had to be silent
run toward the dark
watch the procession of ghosts
listen to a mother eat the entrails of her son
feel his father half-scorpion scatter tumors in his brain.

Go out in the field
give a drink to the *Rompenucas*
smell the earth in the furrows of its hands
stare at the stupidity of resistance
so solitude will not be so sad
in the confusion of this morgue eradicating ancient archives.

IV

a mi madre

Me clama piedad
se levanta resistiendo la ausencia de alimento
intuye que quiero lanzar mi alma por el desagüe
sé que en cualquier momento va a morir
que no soy la que ella quisiera.

Hoy le he dicho
que todo su rostro se parece al de Frida Kahlo
(mira qué guapa)
pero aquí entre nos
el parecido no está sólo en el rostro
también son las bellas trenzas
y el vientre dañado
pues en este complot
yo puedo ser su hija
pero en otro
fui el feto perdido de Frida.

¡Reza! ¡reza por favor!
le grito
y ella reza a no sé quién para tener valor
mientras
esperamos que explote el veneno.

IV

to my mother

She begs for mercy
gets up fighting the absence of food
senses that I want to flush my soul down the drain
I know that any moment she is going to die
that I am not what she was hoping for.

Today I told her
that her face was just like Frida Kahlo's
(look how lovely)
but just between the two of us
the similarity is not only in the face
but also in the lovely braids
and the cursed womb
for in this story
I can be her daughter
but in the other
I was Frida's lost embryo.

Pray! Please pray!
I cry out to her
and she prays I do not know to whom for courage
while
we wait for the poison to explode.

V

Cuando los animales salvajes despiertan
quieren alimentarse de inmortales sin hijos
ver el lápiz del ciego
sentir el abrazo que debería llegar
en los antiguos caballos de totora.

Despiertos
reteniendo la vida
cuentan murmullos desquijados
hacen trenzas en el cabello del choclo
y cosen el vientre de un higo.

Nada les queda en paz
rompen todo
desbaratan la sangre
y en un proyecto se la dan al moribundo
lo resucitan
para luego morder su fémur.

A veces se ofrecen para recibir plegarias
pero es definitivo
cuando se despiertan
sus dientes hierven en la boca de un enfermo.

V

When wild animals awake
they want to feed upon immortals without children
see the blind man's pencil,
feel the embrace that must have come
with those old wicker rafts.

Awake
regaining life
they tell their tales in jaw-breaking whispers
weave braids of corn silk
sew tight the womb of a fig.

They leave nothing in peace
they break everything
they destroy our blood
and give it to the dying as an experiment
they bring him back to life
to bite him shortly after on the femur.

Sometimes they offer to accept our prayers
but for sure
when they awake
their teeth are boiling in a sickened mouth.

VI

Sólo cuando nos obligan a hablar
nos asomamos por los ojos
la boca
las orejas
las manos.

Adentro somos cuervos
nadie escucha nuestro violín
las velas se apagan
en la lengua fluye desnudo un insecto
los pretextos se derrumban tras las columnas

nos hemos sacado la mirada.

VI

Only when they make us speak
do we begin to peer out through our eyes
mouths
ears
hands.

Within we are crows
no one hears our violin
the candles go out
naked an insect flows along my tongue
pretexts collapse behind the columns

we have torn our gaze out by the root.

VII

No doy pie con bola
ni puñete con cara
no sé en qué momento se terminó el día
si conmigo en brazos
sentí que la tristeza no es sólo para los viejos
ataca desde el vientre
pero aún así
busqué esos supuestos amigos
que nos impiden convertirnos
en monstruos tan familiares.

En qué momento
si ya estaba viviendo
con la terquedad de recoger el corazón tirado a la basura
mientras una paloma para salvar la imagen de su pichón
picoteaba su rostro en las llantas de los carros.

Si por navidad
ya compraba una esponja para el baño
si ya les decía:
almas malditas prepárense
la muertita está de pie y bailará en sus tumbas
con la misma voluntad que dan y escuchan misa.

Si desde mi ventana empezaba a husmear dudas de las sombras
disimulando disculpas por los desencuentros.

Si ya estaba completa
muerta con movimientos.
Qué pasó
en qué momento la sangre se me reventó
me empapó
me dejó como cucaracha flaca.

Si me vieran
ahora parezco Buda con su ayuno
desbaratada
casi un agujero rojo estampado en el suelo
y siento que Dios se acerca
pienso que él me recogerá por pedazos

VII

I can't hit the broad side of a barn
I can't tell my ass from my elbow
I don't know at what moment the day ended
if with me in its arms
I felt that sadness isn't only for the old
it attacks from the very womb
yet even so
I looked for those supposed friends
who stop us from becoming
such familiar monsters.

At what moment
if I finally was alive
with the stubbornness of picking my heart out of the garbage
while a dove protecting the image of its young
pecked at its face reflected in hubcaps.

If for Christmas
I were to buy a sponge for the bathroom
if I were to tell them:
damned souls get ready
the little one is on her feet and will dance upon your graves
with the same eagerness you show in saying or in hearing Mass.

If from my window I began to sniff out shadows' doubts
inventing excuses for our failure to meet.

If I was finally complete
dead but still in motion.
What happened
at what moment did my blood explode
leaving me soaked
like a scrawny cockroach.

If they could see me
now looking like a broken
fasting Buddha
almost a red hole stamped in the floor
as I feel God drawing near
thinking he will gather up my pieces

me dará calma
pero mientras más cerca está esa presencia
me doy cuenta que estoy delirando
pues es mi perro que al verme así
también se ha vuelto sangre.

bring me serenity
but the closer his presence comes
the more I realize I'm delirious
because it's my dog that seeing me like this
has also turned to blood.

VIII

"…los muertos queridos, no dejan vivir.
Me llaman sin parar desde la tumba"
— Fernando Vallejo.

En las mañanas de un lugar a otro
y en las noches
colocando en la imaginación
luz
agua
patio
inclusive ya pasaba a la sala
se servía Cantaclaro y pan de Vilcabamba.

Pero ella ya lo había visto
empezó a mostrar su nariz al filo de las puertas:
   — a éste me lo llevo
hay tantos
pero porqué me he de llevar a esas horribles cargas.
¡No!
este es el indicado
¿a dónde me lo llevaré?
Si cree en el infierno
    allá
      si cree en el cielo
      me lo guardo en el bolsillo —

Y él que no se moría
la otra desesperada.
El tiempo lo vistió de cosa secundaria
el sueño se acostumbró a dormir colgado de su cabeza
y a las siete con quince minutos
a la perdida se le hizo el milagro
pues cuando algo patea en el corazón
uno termina podrido.

Mientras respira el reloj de la pared
entre mis manos hay una República del Ecuador
un número de cédula y una falla multisistémica.
Ahora
ya sé a quien se llevó de puntillas esa atrevida
al de la tumba que me reclama como su hija.

VIII

"...the dear departed don't leave us alone.
They call me, endless, from the grave."
— Fernando Vallejo

In the morning from one place to another
and in the evening
arranging in the imagination
light
water
yard
and already she was entering the living room
serving herself Cantaclaro and bread from Vilcabamba.

But she had already seen it
it had begun to show its nose through the cracks of doors
    — I'll take this one
there are so many
but why me to carry such a horrible load.
No!
this is the right one
where should I take it?
If it believes in hell
       over there
       if it believes in heaven
       I'll keep it in my pocket —

And he, the one who didn't die
and she, the other without hope.
Time dressed him as a thing subordinate
dreams grew used to sleeping hanging from his head
and at seven fifteen
the poor thing got her miracle
because when something's kicking in the heart
one ends up rotten to the core.

While the clock breathes on the wall
in my hands there is a Republic of Ecuador
a numbered ID and a multi-systemic failure.
Now
I know who the arrogant one took away on tiptoes
the one in the grave who claims me as his daughter.

IX

Salten como yo
¡bailen!
tomen vodka
vengan con el pastel
hoy celebro mi último cumpleaños
con una calavera en el pensamiento

no se asusten
si al final
sólo quedan
espejos.

IX

Leap like me
dance!
drink vodka
bring in the cake
today I celebrate my final birthday
with a skull in my thoughts.

Don't be afraid
if in the end
all that is left
are mirrors.

X

Absurdamente mis incontables patalean
nacen en el túnel.

Me beben todas las mañanas
me acompañan el resto de siglos
parecemos un cacho tonto vigilados por el tiempo
él
lazarillo de la muerte
ansioso por conocer en qué hombros soltaremos la cabeza.

¿Pero qué hombro puede cargar con nosotros?

Nosotros que desbaratamos cunas
dueños del setenta y ocho por ciento del mundo
la parte que no pone huevos
al lado de los perros y los niños en la calle.

¿Qué hombro?
Si los incontables y Yo
somos los botados en medio de la vía pública.

¿Cuándo una invocación familiar
nos alumbró el alma?
¿Cuándo nos impidieron acercarnos a los espejos?
esas puertas que terminan con la magia
e inician con el mundo real.

¿Cuándo?

Botados coleccionando momentos
en ésta tragicomedia
mientras nos recorre el miedo de morir todavía pequeños
ángeles pálidos
ocultos en los rincones del sueño
que más hiede a insomnio.

Cuándo entenderán las bestias
que los perros y los niños no deben morir
pues el sueño de un niño
va en la espalda de un perro.

X

Absurd my countless ones stamp their feet
they are born in the tunnel.

They drink me every morning
they accompany me through all the centuries that are left
we seem foolish fragments watched over by Time
yes he
Death's *lazarillo*, his blind man's guide,
eager to know from which shoulders we will take a head.

But what shoulder can bear to carry us?

We, wreckers of cradles
lords of seventy-eight percent of the world
the part that doesn't leave bones
beside the dogs and children in the street.

What shoulder?
If it's the countless ones and I
dumped in the middle of the public road.

When did a familiar invocation
bring light to our soul?
When did they prevent us from approaching mirrors?
those doors that end in magic
and begin with the real world.

When?

Dumped there collecting moments
in this tragicomedy
while through us runs the fear of dying while still pale
little angels
hidden in the corners of a sleep
reeking with insomnia.

When will the beasts understand
that dogs and children shouldn't die
for the dream of a child
rides on a dog's back.

¡Dios!
ya no sé cuántas veces te he llamado
los niños deberíamos escuchar cuentos
en los que el águila salva al conejo de la hiena.
¡Dios!
en la lengua de los humanos nos regalaste.

Mis incontables nacen en el túnel
y yo al visitarme
me veo arrodillada ante el Señor de la Mancha
visceralmente llorando sentencias.

God!
I don't know how many times I've called to you
we children ought to hear stories
in which the eagle saves the rabbit from the hyena.
God!
you have regaled us in a human tongue.

My countless ones are born in the tunnel
and I, visited,
see myself kneeling before the Man of La Mancha
viscerally weeping out judgment.

XI

Bienvenido al atardecer de este mundo
aquí estamos sentados en el horizonte
los reyes tristes
los únicos que podemos traspasar
todos los decibeles de la felicidad.

Bienvenido a los ojos
a los estanques de nuestros muertos que nunca se van.

Bienvenido a este valle de ausencias
al frío en las manos.

Bienvenido a nuestra cuna sin padres
al vientre en donde sólo las aves fénix pueden nacer
para "gobernar en el infierno
antes que servir en la gloria".

Bienvenido al muelle
donde los ingenuos escribimos detrás de un diagnóstico clínico
donde la vida festeja las cosquillas del viento.

Bienvenido a los inmortales del insomnio.
Bienvenido a nosotros
fantasma gris del silencio.

XI

Welcome to the twilight of this world
here we are seated on the horizon
the sad kings
the only ones who can go beyond
all the decibels of happiness.

Welcome to the eyes
standing pools of our dead who never go away.

Welcome to this valley of absences
to the cold of these hands.

Welcome to our cradle without parents
to the womb from which only a phoenix can be born
to "reign in hell
rather than serve in glory."

Welcome to the dock
where we the ingenuous write from behind our clinical diagnoses
where life celebrates the teasing of the wind.

Welcome to the immortals of insomnia.
Welcome to us
gray ghost of silence.

ERRORS OF THE WINDOWS

LOS ERRORES DE LAS VENTANAS

El cuerpecillo desventrado y fláccido de la tórtola no llena la carie de un diente de Dios

The body of the turtle-dove, small, eviscerated, flaccid, doesn't fill the cavity in one of God's teeth

— José Saramago

XII

Nunca fue fácil verte desde esta vereda
en medio de misiles
de fosas.

Te busco entre huesos
ojos
rodillas

y hay tantos...

Ven
antes que un Franco/tirador
declare también culpable a tu sombra.

Hay tantos.
pero te busco
eres vos
tu cráneo está entre mis manos.

XII

It was never easy to see you from this path
there amidst missiles
and mass graves.

I search for you among bones
eyes
knees

there are so many…

Come
before some Franco/marksman
proclaims your ghost is guilty, too.

There are so many
but I search for you
you
your skull between my hands.

XIII

Muerto querendón de Dios
Tus buitres me persiguen.

La refrigeradora
fantasma con electricidad habla en las noches.

Un ombligo se cae frente al semáforo.

Ya no hay sombras vigías.

Mi cabeza vagabunda
te dice que no debes dormir temprano
porque con ese cuento de la cama
nos entrenan para la correcta utilización del ataúd.

Muerto querendón de Dios
me he liberado de él
me gusta la vida con pájaros al final del cuarto de grillos.

Muerto de un metro setenta centímetros
mi endriago
eres el más muerto de toda tu familia.

Muerto sordo
mi memoria empieza a tener polillas
ya no sé cuál era la esquina del ojo atento
no sé en qué mano de la paz esté con vosotros
dejé botado mi nombre
no recuerdo a qué hora
debo tomar los calmantes.

Muerto corriente
ya no tienes puntos cardinales.

Muerto querendón de Dios
el ladrón amontonado a la derecha
ya no puede salvarte
peor devolverte la infancia
para que juegues en ésta
mi rayuela mal hecha.

XIII

Dead man cherisher of God
your vultures chase me down.

The phantom fridge
speaks electric through the night.

A navel falls before the traffic light.

There are no longer any watching shadows.

My vagrant head
warns you not to fall asleep too soon
for with this business of the bed
they're teaching us the proper way to use our coffin.

Dead man cherisher of God
I've freed myself from him
I like life with birds at the back of the room of shackles.

Dead man nearly six feet tall
my fabled monster
you're the deadest of your whole family.

Dead man deaf
moths begin to eat away my memory
I no longer know which was the corner of my attentive eye
I don't know in which hand peace may be with you
I threw my name away
I don't remember when
I'm supposed to take my pills.

Dead like all the others
you no longer know north from south.

Dead man cherisher of God
the thief hanging to your right
can no longer save you
or even bring you back to childhood
so you can play hop-scotch
on my crooked squares.

XIV

Te he sacrificado.
La ciudad está desinflada
dos pichones con alas harapientas rezan conmigo.

¡Dios! ¿Qué Dios está detrás de ti?
tus hijos respiran en mi estómago
me los comí de desesperación
al sentir que el espermatozoide
cruzaba los límites de la paciencia.

Perdón
te he sacrificado
como a todos los que se han acercado
mi culpa
es mi culpa
pero de qué me sirve
si el día de los espíritus muertos llega cada mes
 y ellos me reclaman sus tumbas
quieren ponérselas
y Yo
sólo puedo mirarme los ojos.

XIV

I've sacrificed you.
The city's gone flat
two pigeons with ragged wings are praying with me.

God! What God stands behind you?
your children are breathing in my stomach
I ate them in desperation
feeling that the spermatozoid
was crossing the limits of my patience.

Forgive me
I've sacrificed you
as I have all those who have come close
my guilt
is my guilt
but what good is it
if the day of the dead comes each month
and they reclaim from me their graves
to put them on again
and I
can only stare into my eyes.

XV

Ella pide monedas para el cemento
se guarda la mañana
y la tarde la arroja al azar.

Tartamudea frente a un fulano
al que no le interesan causas perdidas.

Medio abrazada a la vida
nunca se queja en el letargo viscoso de una fábula.

XV

... She wore a burning blouse
She had eyes to rock the sea to sleep
She'd hidden a dream in a dark closet
and found a dead man in the middle of her head...
— Vicente Huidobro

She begs coins for cement
keeps the morning for herself
and throws the afternoon to chance.

She stammers to some guy
who isn't interested in lost causes.

Half embracing life
she never complains in the viscous lethargy of a fable.

XVI

El día que comenzaste a quedar en silencio
mi padre en el cartón de su ropa
traía el aliento de los amantes enterrados.

Callada supe
cómo el fémur cruje debajo de las hojas.

Este mes
ese padre mío dejará a los de Sumpa
saldrá de la llaga
bajo el brazo llevará sus restos
mientras yo por las calles
llevaré a tu hijo en el cerebro.

XVI

That day you began to grow silent
my father in his box of clothes
brought along the breath of buried lovers.

Silent I knew
how the femur crackles beneath the leaves.

This month
that father of mine will leave behind those Sumpa lovers
escape his sores
and beneath his arm will carry their remains
while I carry through the streets
your son here in my brain.

XVII

Esto de quedarse viendo a la luna
es como haber perdido a un recién nacido
que poco a poco ya nos iba distinguiendo del resto
que ya empezaba a entender de que pata cojeábamos.

Esto de quedarse viendo a la luna
es como rezar sin abrir la boca
es como cruzar los dedos ante la incertidumbre
es poner a practicar a los ojos
la mirada que no se ha de dar
para conservar la prudencia.

Esto de quedarse viendo a la luna
es un peligro
porque mientras estamos con cara de enfermos
que padecemos los adioses de lejos
nos puede dar un mal aire
o lo más probable
un mal de ojo.

Esto de quedarse viendo a la luna
es cosa seria
es como si nos hubiéramos
quedado para siempre en la tierra
clasificando los latidos con lágrimas secas.

XVII

This business of simply gazing at the moon
is like having lost a newborn child
who has just begun to tell us from the rest
who has begun, in fact, to know our weaknesses.

This business of simply gazing at the moon
is like praying without opening your mouth
like crossing your fingers when in doubt
like rehearsing with your eyes
a look you never ought to give
for the sake of modesty.

This business of simply gazing at the moon
is dangerous
for while we stand there with a sick look on our face
suffering farewells from far away
it could lead us toward malaise
or even worse
the evil eye.

This business of simply gazing at the moon
is a serious thing
it's as if we'd stayed
on earth forever
measuring out heartbeats with desiccated tears.

XVIII

En tu cuerpo van todas las lujurias de un pueblo.
Anteojudo pasas
clavando los dientes en la insolación
creyendo que de un ojo
varias retinas te guardan.

En tu cuerpo van todas las lujurias de un pueblo
pasas construyendo una torre
con piedras de un cielo vacío.

Tu blancura ha de arder un día
pasarás por mi sombra hasta tu carne
desde mis mil enfermedades
hasta tu una y mil codicias
desde mi boca que la quieres callada
hasta el temblor de tus huesos.

Todo arderá
desde mi vestuario de tumba
hasta vos
bello pájaro de porcelana.

Pobre invento mío
siempre huirás por todos lados
llevando en tu cuerpo
todas las lujurias de un pueblo.

XVIII

Through your body flow all the yearnings of a people.
Behind your glasses you walk by
sinking your teeth into sun-stroke
believing that from a single eye
various retinas are watching over you.

Through your body flow all the yearnings of a people.
You spend your time building a tower
with stones from an empty sky.

Some day your whiteness will burn away
you will pass through my shadow to your flesh
from my thousand maladies
to your thousand and one shades of avarice
from my mouth you wish were silent
to the trembling of your bones.

Everything will burn
from my burial clothes
to you
my beautiful porcelain bird.

My poor invention
you will always flee in all directions
carrying in your body
all the yearnings of a people.

XIX

Otra vez ha encontrarme
en la cosa seria que es la planicie del campo.
Cuántos andrajos se habrá puesto esta vieja
cuántas veces el patíbulo del reloj dio la vuelta.
Cuántas veces el sol brilló en una lágrima
mientras los académicos criticaban nuestras trilladas quejas
pues ni bien escritas estaban.
Pero qué se podía hacer:
las palabras no salían esdrújulas
a puro remojo con palo se notaban graves.

Encontrada entre varios
se han multiplicado sin conciencia
raza mal ubicada
no deja espacio a los animales
a los que llevan el corazón en los ojos.

Raza aprovechada
los nuestros se van
y en la despedida tragamos estrellas.
Encontrada para qué
si ahora la muerte me da miedo
antes la invitaba a desayunar
pero ahora me da miedo su pastilla tras pastilla.

Sé que allá nadie espera
pero esto sólo lo entiendo en la batalla final.

¿Encontrada y muerta?
por lo menos si lo hiciera como mi padre
que toda su vida se la pasó de bueno
y al final fue vengativo
no les dejó ni medio centímetro de carne a los gusanos
pues se pudrió en vida.

Encontrada y qué
que nadie se apunte en la lista
ni abrazos ni tabacos daré
sólo a mi grupo de muertos hablaré

XIX

Once again I find myself
on that serious thing, the surface of the earth.
How many rags has that old woman put on
how often has the scaffold of the clock gone round.
How often has the sun glistened in a tear
while academics criticized our hackneyed plaints
for they weren't even written well.
But what could one do:
words did not come out accented as they should
only after a beating did the meter come out right.

Found amongst many
who have multiplied without conscience
an ill-placed race
leaving no room for animals
those who carry their heart in their eyes.

Opportunistic race
those who are our own are going away
and as we say farewell we swallow stars.
Found for what reason
if death now frightens me
while before I invited it to breakfast
yes now it frightens me pill by pill.

I know no one awaits me there
but I understand this only in the final battle.

Found and dead?
at least if I can do it like my father
who all his life was good
and turned vindictive at the end
not leaving half a centimeter of flesh for the worms
since he'd turned rotten still in life.

Found and so what?
may no one put himself on the list
I will give neither hugs nor cigarettes
will only speak to my own circle of the dead

sólo a los míos rezaré
y como un perro le dice a otro vamos al parque
a mis muertos les diré:
vamos por el callejón
hacia la noche que siempre espera
a los que aman de pie.

will pray to my own alone
and like a dog saying to another dog lets go to the park
to my dead I'll say:
lets go down the alley
to the night that always waits
for those who do their loving standing up.

DRAWER
FULL OF NOISE

CAJON DE RUIDOS

*No te asustes si un día encuentras un esqueleto
viviendo dentro de ti.*

Don't be surprised if one day you find a skeleton
living inside you

Insomnio

Es una mancha que ingiere lunas
trae pensamientos que dejan a cualquiera fuera del cuerpo
uno los ve de lejos
algunas veces dan vueltas
se tropiezan unos con otros
discuten
se cortan las venas
cuando se calman
testarudos y aburridos se sientan
unen sus puños
para golpear a alguien.

Esta mancha comunica a los cuartos
con sus respectivos silencios
luego nos incorpora un terremoto
que pasa de las manos a los ojos.
Arsenical llena la cama
saca las velas
las engorda para su descendencia.

Nunca pone en remojo a los minutos
los deja como son: piedras
que lanzadas a una noche de afuera
hacen maullar a los gatos.

Ella en su inmortalidad
se burla de las pastillas de valeriana
y poco a poco
se va preñando
amenaza con traer a seres que debajo de sus sombreros
siempre tienen tabacos armables
que hacen desaparecer
cualquier calambre vencido de sueño.

Insomnia

It is a stain that feeds on moons
brings thoughts that leave you outside your body
you see them from afar
sometimes they spin around
they bump into each other
argue
cut their veins
when they calm down
they sit there obstinate and annoyed
they clench their fists
to hit someone.

This stain spreads to the rooms
with their respective silences
then plants in us an earthquake
that passes from our hands to our eyes.
Arsenic fills the bed
brings out the candles
swells them for her descendents.

Never place minutes to soak
leave them as they are: stones
that thrown at the night outside
make cats howl.

She in her immortality
mocks the valerian pills
and bit by bit
she grows pregnant
threatens to bring forth beings who beneath their big hats
always have their rolling tobacco
that makes any spasm
defeated by sleep disappear.

No hay como confiar en los sensibles

son complicados
cuando hablan nadie los entiende.

Están claros en el dolor
lloran cuando ven a la humanidad
sus ojos se enredan en las respiraciones.
Están en todo y no están en nada.
Cuando se callan parece que están serenos
pero en realidad sus pensamientos están desordenados
se repiten las cosas hasta convertirlas en fuego.

Cuando se deciden a vivir
encuentran muertos en su cabeza
y caminan por las calles apretando los labios.

Como niños silenciosos se sientan a contemplar el horizonte
parece que algo se les va a reventar en el pecho
y sin fijarse en lenguas mal intencionadas
ponen sus ojos frente al suelo
como obligándole al cemento a responder los mil porqués.

Estos seres son insoportables
-eso dicen todos-
les molesta su existencia
ni su propia sombra los aguanta
nunca ponen en venta sus sueños
siempre están en huída
abrazando toda forma de soledad.

Aunque no lo dicen
no soportan los hastaluegos
cuando los visitan
se sumergen en el terror
y en su metro de espacio
lloran como huérfanos en medio del mundo.

No hay como confiar en los sensibles
fingen ser de hierro
pero sólo una caricia o un soplo en la cabeza
les basta para romperse entre nuestras manos
se quedan como muecas sangrientas
y nos hacen sentir seres frívolos
incapaces de amarlos.

There's Nothing Like Confiding in the Sensitive

they're complicated
when they speak no one understands them.

They're lucid in their pain
they cry when they see humanity
their eyes are tangled in their breaths.
They're in everything and nothing.
When they grow silent they seem to be serene
but in truth their thoughts are chaotic
things repeat themselves until they turn to flames.

When they decide to live
they find the dead in their heads
and so they walk the streets lips pressed tight together.

Like silent children they sit there contemplating the horizon
it's as if something's going to burst within their chests
and paying no regard to painful words
they fix their eyes upon the ground
as if forcing the cement to answer their one thousand whys.

These creatures are unbearable
that's what everyone says--
their own existence troubles them
their own shadows can't stand them
they never try to sell their dreams
they're always running away
embracing any form of solitude.

Although they don't say so
they cannot bear those see-you-laters
when people visit them
they are immersed in terror
and in their one square metered space
they cry like orphans in the middle of the world.

There's nothing like confiding in the sensitive
they pretend to be of steel
but a mere caress and a breath on their head
is enough for them to fall to pieces in our hands
and with god-awful grimaces
they make us feel as if we're frivolous
incapable of loving them.

Las palabras

Ahora que las veo me dan miedo
pues con el transcurso del tiempo
se han vuelto tan inestables
ya no se aguantan en remojo hasta el otro día
antes de dormir piden andar por el papel
amenazan
se voltean a mirarme
me ponen de rodillas
me desafían con la verdad.

Las peores
las no dichas en público
parecen gatos colgados de mi boca
están en todo
por ejemplo
un día observaba en silencio unas fotografías
y sin llamarlas vinieron
me gritaron al oído:
¡Ehy! ¡Qué haces con muertos secos!

¡Ah, estas palabras!

Se ríen porque saben en qué tiempo y ante qué ventana
con tabaco en mano me empujaron a un latido negro.

Señoras
me dan miedo cuando se van a mi garganta
y casi no puedo respirar.
Cuando digo ustedes son mías
y se convierten en palabrotas
y dicen de que madre he nacido.

Words

Now that I see them I'm afraid
for with the passing of time
they have become so unstable
they no longer can stand to soak till the next day
before going to sleep they ask if they can walk about the page
they make threats
they turn to stare at me
they force me to my knees
they confront me with the truth.

The worst of all
the ones not said in public
seem like cats dangling from my mouth
they're everywhere
for example
one day I was looking in silence at some photographs
and without my calling they came
they screamed in my ear:
Hey! What are you doing with the dried-out dead!

Ah, those words!

They laugh because they know at what time and facing what window,
cigarette in hand, they'll push me to a black heartbeat.

Ladies
they frighten me when they rise in my throat
and I can barely breathe.
When I say to them you all are mine
and they change to curses
and ask me who's my mother.

El ser que han buscado debió caerse en alguna parte

no está aquí
he revisado mi rostro
y la mancha de la frente
es producto del sarampión
los lunares son por el sol de la tarde
y mis ojos están llenos de polvo.

He visto mi estatura frente al espejo
me examiné sin zapatos
y soy más pequeña cuando miro al Este.

Estoy con náuseas
una espada me atraviesa la gastritis
tengo una alergia que se cae.
Es verdad
mi rostro no compagina con las costillas.

Me he visto y no me parezco
busquen a otro ser
porque quien me habita
es un inconsolable
que cada noche opta por el suicidio tras la puerta del baño.

The One They've Been Looking For Must Have Fallen Through a Crack

she isn't here
I've examined my face
and the mark on my brow
is just from the measles
the other spots are from the afternoon sun
and my eyes are filled with dust.

I've checked my height in the mirror
considered myself without shoes on
and I'm smaller when I'm looking East.

I'm nauseous
a sword cuts me through, gastritis
I have an allergy descending.
It's true
my face doesn't match my ribs.

I have seen myself and I don't look like me
seek another self
for the one that dwells inside me
is someone inconsolable
choosing suicide every night behind the bathroom door.

He buscado a los muertos entre los vivos

y el corazón me ha latido sin respuestas
si pudiera saber qué les ronda
cuándo miran las flores
cuándo se hacen fuego
cuándo el silencio raspa sus palabras.

He buscado a los muertos
mientras el vino me ha empapado la cara
mientras la noche
se ha caído al filo de la batalla...

derrota
derrota

pero ningún muerto mío se ha ido derrotado
por eso los busco
por valientes
pues en algún lugar deben estar multiplicándose
haciéndose verdad
haciéndose fruto
pero dónde
a dónde más ir...

Si mis muertos no están con los otros muertos
si mis muertos tampoco están con los vivos
si mis muertos aún no se han ido
si mis muertos son niños...

¿Dónde están?
¿la soledad se los tragaría?
¿la muy obesa les habrá tomado fotos?
¿será que allí están estampados?

dónde
dónde...

Será que un vivo nunca puede llegar a los oídos de un muerto
será que hay que conocer el mapa del cementerio
para dar con la resignación exacta...

Busco sin encontrar
¿y cruzar lo incierto?
¿si los gusanos me comen sin dudar...?

I Have Sought the Dead Among the Living

while my heart beat on without reply.
If only I could know what hovers round them
when they gaze at flowers
when they turn to fire
when silence scratches out their words.

I have sought the dead
while wine soaked my face
while night
fell to the blade of battle...

defeat
defeat

but not one of my dead has been defeated
that's why I seek them
for their valor
since somewhere they must be reproducing
turning to truth
turning to fruit
but where
where else can I go...

If my dead are not with the other dead
if my dead are not with the living either
if my dead have not yet gone
if my dead are children...

Where are they?
could solitude have devoured them?
could the fat one have taken their picture?
could they be caught in those prints?

where
where...

Could it be a living person can never reach the ears of the dead
could it be one has to know the map of the cemetery
in order to come upon one's perfect resignation...

I seek and do not find
and should I enter the uncertain
if worms will eat me free of doubt...?

El siguiente paso será el último

pero la cenicienta en la esquina
las cartas leídas e intactas
los juguetes lúcidos desde un baúl.

El siguiente paso será el último.
De la pared salen nombres sin cabeza
la verdad conspira en los ojos
hay arañas de vino
el corazón cada día está más torcido...

El siguiente paso será el último.
Los amigos están mejor en las manos de otros
la leche materna se ahoga en un pozo
la noche exhorta tabacos como estrellas
por cada dedo una pastilla
por cada muela podrida una sonrisa menos en el espejo
pero ésta vez sí
el siguiente paso es el último.

La esperanza nunca fue verde
ser inocente es opcional
los recuerdos nos maldicen con la cara del tiempo.

El siguiente paso es el último
pero hay que comer
bañarse
dormir
y dormir es morirse
y en esta nueva cortina afrodisíaca
de qué cuerpo hablarán los muertos
si ninguno es conveniente.

Y así/aun casi/tan sólo si/por poco/
pero en este truco de ser esqueleto con respiración
luego del penúltimo paso
hubo que vivir como sea.

The Next Step Will Be the Last

but Cinderella in the corner
cards read and left untouched
her toys lucid in their trunk.

The next step will be the last.
From the wall names without faces emerge
truth conspires in my eyes
there are spiders in the wine
the heart grows more twisted every day...

The next step will be the last.
Our friends are better off in the hands of others
mother's milk drowns in a well
the night calls forth tobacco like stars
for each finger a pill
for each rotten tooth one less smile in the mirror
but this time yes
the next step will be the last.

Hope was never green
to be innocent is optional
memories damn us with the face of time.

The next step will be the last
but one has to eat
to wash
to sleep
and to sleep is to die
and in this new aphrodisiacal curtain
which body will the dead discuss
if there isn't one that fits.

And so/yet nearly/if only/almost
but in this trick of being a skeleton that breathes
after the penultimate step
one had to live as best one could.

Nadie puede creer la edad que nos recorre

la fatiga que nos ahuyenta de las reuniones
pero nosotros creemos en este falso mirador de cometas...

Gestos se acercan
cuando decimos maldita sangre
maldita conciencia
parece que a este mundo
el dolor no le queda.

Se fastidian con la verdad las máscaras.

¿Qué se puede hacer con el niño
que nace soñando con la muerte?
¿Besar su frente?
¿Arropar sus huesos?
¿Llevarlo en el conjunto de papeles sin rostro?

Por ser autistas
el predicado futuro es el manicomio
y ningún erario sufrirá de inanición
como ningún alcalde de la soberbia
salvará a la madre
convertida en una más de los sobrevivientes
a los que por cada ojo les sale otro sin infancia.

En esta edad de "guaguas"
no deberíamos padecer de licantropía
ni exiliarnos para cuidar flores
ni dormirnos con fotografías
pues vuela el peligro que en cualquier momento
los diarios publiquen: estos seres apestan.

Pero no hay otrora
así hemos de quedarnos
los elegidos
los malditos
con un puñal atravesado en el silencio.

Who Could Believe the Times We're Living In

the exhaustion that drives us from our meetings
but we believe in this false lookout point for comets...

Gestures draw closer
when we say damned blood
accursed consciousness
it's like this world's too small for all our pain.

Masks are bored with the truth.

What can one do with the child
born dreaming of death?
Kiss his forehead
Tuck in his bones?
Carry him in a stack of faceless papers?

For the autistic
the obvious future is the asylum
and no public treasury gives a damn about starvation
just as no pretentious mayor
is going to help some mother
seen as just another survivor
spawning another brat without a childhood at the blink an eye.

In this age of babes in arms
we shouldn't have to deal with lycanthropy
or leave our damned country for a bunch of flowers
or use a photograph to get some sleep
just because there's the risk that at any moment
the newspapers will say: these creatures are a plague.

But there's no time to waste
this is how it has to be:
the chosen
the damned
with a dagger thrust through silence.

Yo no escribo porque otros escribieron antes

¡No!
escribo porque me tocaron horas raras
en las que uno presiente la muerte
el miedo
eso de quedarse invisible
y suicidarse frente al resto.
Horas en que sabes que naciste para Lucifer
y que como él has de tambalear por el mundo
luego del encuentro con el alcohol.

Yo no escribo porque otros escribieron antes de mí.
Escribo porque me enteré que estaba viva
y entonces fui al parque a ver a la gente pasar como palomas.

Escribo para mí
para el resto.
Escribo una denuncia
un reclamo
unas preguntas:
¿dónde está tu espalda?
¿dónde estamos…?

Escribo aunque sea sólo un existencialismo de esquina.

Escribo algo
porque uno también es el séptimo Juan sin Cielo
el lugar común
porque a uno también lo torturaron.
Disque por Dios
a uno también le tocó ser un crucificado
una bruja —manzana perfecta— en la hoguera.

Escribo a mis plumajes
a las lunas que caían sobre la casa
al pasto donde por primera y última vez me arrodillé
a la noche más negra y larga.
Al viento que me anticipaba la danza de buitres
a la flor que hace tiempo murió
a la música que se acuesta a los pies de mi cama
a mi padre que fue un niño
a la pólvora que me empujó al tabaco a la una de la mañana

I Don't Write Because Others Wrote Before

No!
I write because strange moments have touched me
when I've had presentiments of death
of fear
that business of growing invisible
and killing oneself in front of everyone.
Moments when you know that you were born for Lucifer
and that just like him you have to stagger through the world
after a meeting with alcohol.

I don't write because others wrote before me.
I write because I came to see I was alive
and so I went to the park to watch the people going by like pigeons.

I write for me
for all the others.
I write denunciations
a complaint
some questions:
where is your back?
where are we?

I write even if it's just street corner existentialism.

I write something
because we too are sad sack,
a commonplace
because we've been torturers as well.
Supposedly in the name of God
it's your turn to be crucified as well
a witch —a perfect apple— on the bonfire.

I write to my plumage
to the moons that fell upon the house
to the pasture where for the first and last time I knelt down
to the deepest darkest night.
To the wind that heralded the dance of the vultures
to the flower that long ago died
to the music that lies at the foot of my bed
to my father who was once a child
to the gunpowder that pushed me to smoke at one in the morning

al grito de no me abandones
a la sangre que obstruye mis venas
a las manos que aullaron como perros sin dueño
al payaso que llora frente al espejo
al papel que en media alba sólo responde verdades
a la foto cuando uno todavía fingía inocencia
a todo lo que me permite alzar esta copa en las tinieblas

Escribo
no porque otros hayan escrito antes
disculpen mi arrogancia
pero es cierto
yo escribo borracha
unas veces llorando de alegría
y otras gimiendo ceniza.

No escribo por humilde
ni mucho menos para liberarme de mis muertos
es decir de mis fantasmas
es decir de mis únicas compañías.
¡No!
Escribo porque detesto el olvido
porque no encuentro nada más que hacer en mi agenda:
cajón de ruidos.

to the cry of don't leave me
to the blood that clogs my veins
to the hands that howled like dogs without masters
to the clown who cries before the mirror
to the sheet of paper that in the midst of dawn only gives back truths
to the photo where one still pretended innocence
to all that lets me lift this cup in the dark.

I write
not because others have written before me
excuse my arrogance
but what's for sure
I write drunkenly
sometimes crying for joy
sometimes moaning ashes.

I don't write from humility
even less to free myself of my dead
that is to say my only companions.
No!
I write because I detest oblivion
because I can't find anything else to do in my agenda:
that drawer full of noise.

PANDEMONIUM

PANDEMONIUM

el mundo se acostumbró a oler a infierno

the world grew used to the stench of hell

A

Anoche vinieron los diablos
besaban la ventana
alargaban las manos
querían arrastrarme.

Cerraba los ojos
pero uno con curiosidad saltona
me los volvía a abrir
otros comenzaban a enredarse
mi cabeza volteó para verlos
y ya no estaban.

Se metieron en el calor de los huesos
confundieron mi circulación
la vida estaba bailando en los oídos.

En lugar de corazón
colocaron piedras que aplastaban mi cerebro
gritaban: ¡muerte! ¡muerte!
un sueño que quería palpar

Hoy que narro esta visita
me doy cuenta
que no fue suficiente
que nos hayan dado bastante
de aquello y de lo otro
encima
tenemos inmortalidad.

A

At night the demons came
kissed the window
stretched out their hands
tried to drag me away.

I shut my eyes
but one of them with macabre curiosity
forced them open
others began to surround me
my head turned to see them
and already they were gone

They entered the warmth of my bones
disturbed my circulation
life was dancing in my ears.

Instead of a heart
they filled me with stones that crushed my brain
shouting: death! death!
a dream I wanted to touch.

Today as I tell of this visit
I realize
it wasn't enough
for on top of plenty
of this and that
we're stuck with immortality.

B

Mis perros siempre están con residuos
diurnos y nocturnos
con una pata en el sol
o caminando tristes con sus orejas canceladas.

Se preguntan: qué habrá sido primero
el huevo, la gallina, el gallo o ellos
sienten que existen en una guerra tibia
mientras rompen el diccionario de antónimos
comen un kilo de papel con esferos
y la garganta les empieza a escribir.

Mis perros beben vino para conjugar el aliento
son vivos a palos
entran y salen del conglomerado de sarna
no los llama nadie
porque dicen que son raros
sí
lo son
pues no comen gatos
y están cansados de ladrar.

B

My dogs always have some leftovers
diurnal and nocturnal
with a paw in the sun
or walking sadly along, ears annulled.

They ask themselves: what came first
the egg, the chicken, the rooster or they themselves
they feel they're in a tepid war
as they tear apart the dictionary of antonyms
eat a couple of pounds of paper with pens
and their throats begin to write.

My dogs drink wine to merge their breaths
alive with blows
they come and go from the mangy crowd
no one calls them
they say that they're strange
yes
they are
for they don't eat cats
and they're tired of barking.

C

Esto es un abrupto
donde solamente yerbajo crece
las paredes aplastan canciones
y las fotografías no gradúan el suicidio.

Ni el todo ni el poco se vinieron conmigo.

Con la neblina propia de los lentes
los ojos con su berrueco
las manos con sus planos de heridas
uno es un hilo con la nadería del espejo.

Acostarse despacio
para que el sueño no se vaya
pero aunque uno intente de todo
la sábana abraza un búho.

Los pájaros intentan traer noticias
pero sólo llega una pluma…

La sed enloquece
y el grifo cierne hastaluegos
que pasan a ser recuerdos
esos amigos y enemigos
que no proponen olvido
van subiendo desde el estómago
para convertirse en lágrimas de rutina.

¿Cárcel?
lo resumiría en minutología pausada
en la que el exilio me fuma
sabiendo que duele
porque aún quedan las ganas de volver.

Porque me expulsaron conmigo
pero no con lo mío.

C

A gulley
where only weeds grow
and here the walls crush songs
and the photographs don't measure up to suicide.

Neither the all nor the little came with me.

With the fog of the glasses themselves
eyes with their cataracts
hands with their wounded maps
one is a thread in the nothing of the mirror .

To lie down slowly
so sleep won't go away
but no matter what one tries
the sheets embrace an owl.

The birds try to bring news
but only a feather gets through…

Thirst drives one mad
and the faucet drips good-byes
that turn to memories
those friends and enemies
that don't suggest oblivion
but rising from the stomach
are turned to routine tears.

Prison?
I would sum it up in slow minutologia
in which exile smokes away at me
knowing that it hurts
for the yearning to return still remains.

For they banished me with myself
but not with what was mine.

D

a mi padre

¿Sigues siendo puntual?
¿Sigues comiendo pan en las tardes?
¿Qué hiciste con tus pecas?
¿Hoy volviste a madrugar?
¿Te sigue doliendo el cuerpo?
¿Todavía te jode el salario?
¿Sigues muriendo cuando caminas?
¿Qué fue del perro?
¿Te gustó la limonada del almuerzo?
¿Todavía esperas la voz de tu hermano?
¿Cuántos subterráneos encuentras en ese libro?
¿Qué pasó con tu memoria?
¿Cambiaste de nombre?
¡Contesta por favor!
¿Qué haces aquí
con ese foco en el cuello
alumbrando esta calle?

D

to my father

Are you still on time?
Are you still eating bread in the afternoon?
What have you done with your freckles?
Did you get up early again today?
Does your body still ache all over?
Do you still have that same old fucking salary?
Do you still feel like dying when you walk?
What happened to the dog?
Did you enjoy your lemonade at lunch?
Are you still waiting for your brother's voice?
How many labyrinths have you found in this book?
What's happened to your memory?
Have you changed your name?
Please answer!
What are you doing here
with that floodlight in your neck
lighting up the street?

E

Ahora entiendo a los perros
tener un hueso atravesado en la garganta
es cosa seria.
Dios no puede imaginar
los huesos derramados
en este valle de egolatría.

Huesos anoréxicos
algunos desnutridos por miedo
de caer en el gordo pecado de la gula
otros ya son fantasmas por mucha necesidad
amarillos de tanta espera
muertos por capricho en la hierba.

Duele hasta el hueso esta mala suerte...

El pensamiento se hace flaco
y menciona que el amor es duro de roer
es ahí cuando comprendo a los perros
un hueso atravesado
no te deja respirar
y el fastidio se hace mayor
cuando ese hueso es el tuyo
y astillado se esconde en la hora exacta.

E

Now I understand dogs
to have a bone stuck in your throat
is a serious matter.
God himself couldn't imagine
the bones spilled
in this valley of self-idolatry.

Anorexic bones
emaciated by fear
of succumbing to the massive sin of gluttony
other bones already ghosts from utter poverty
yellow from such long waiting
dead by caprice in the grass.

It aches to the very bone this evil destiny…

Thought grows thin
and remarks that love is hard to gnaw at
that's when I understand the dogs
a bone that's stuck
doesn't let you breathe
and the suffering is even greater
when that bone is yours
and splintered disappears just when you need it.

F

Ayer sufrió de nervios
y ahora
el borracho está bajo la cama
diciendo que su familia lo hizo palillo de dientes
balbucea en calcomanía
el escándalo de llevar una estaca
entre la carne y el esternón
pues según el testimonio de su presencia
lo confundieron con vampiro
siendo amante.

Le atraviesa la mañana
escondido bajo la cama
declarándose cuerdo
para dejar de vivir en un hospital psiquiátrico.

Se le revienta algo
-se revienta-
tal vez esta noche
nos reventemos por completo.

F

Yesterday he was all nerves
and now
the drunk is under the bed
saying his family has turned him into a toothpick
he babbles in caricature
of the scandal of having a stake
thrust through flesh and sternum
since due to the proof of his presence
they confused him, a lover,
with a vampire.

The morning pierces him through
hidden beneath the bed
declaring himself sane
so he can leave this psychiatric ward.

Something explodes inside him
—he explodes—
perhaps tonight
all of us will blow ourselves to bits.

PERROS DE TABACO: CODA

Hoy
este perro después de terminar su jornada
no irá a dormir en su cartón
otra vez correrá hacia lo que todos dicen ya tener.

En la calle los carros lo golpearán
mientras los humanos irán por la vereda
de dos en dos.

Bailará con la soledad
y beberá con aquella que nadie quiere:
la muerte.

La neblina caerá
y nuevamente Sísifo intentará renunciar a su piedra.

En la madrugada
cansado
sentirá el abismo
y como un mendigo ciego
arrastrará su cuerpo hacia el sueño

Como siempre
dará tres vueltas dentro de su pequeño espacio
y llorará como si fuera el único animal abandonado.

Nunca más dirá
pero mientras tenga vida
sabe que cometerá otros desatinos.

Maldito perro
necio
después de esta jornada
entre el frío y el tránsito
hambriento
volverás a buscar
lo que la cabeza
llama amor.

TOBACCO DOGS: CODA

Today
this dog after finishing his work
will not go to sleep in his carton
but once again will run after what everyone says they already have.

In the street cars will batter him
while humans stroll the sidewalk
two by two.

He will dance with solitude
and drink with the one whom no one yearns for:
death.

Fog will fall
and once again Sisyphus will try to leave his stone.

At dawn
exhausted
he will feel the abyss
and like a beggar, blind,
will drag his body off to sleep.

As always
he will turn three times in his small space
and cry as if he were the only abandoned animal

Never again he'll say
but as long as he's alive
he knows he'll be committing other stupid blunders.

Cursed foolish
dog
after this day of work
between the cold and traffic
starving
you will once again go out to search
for what the head
calls love.

ABOUT THE POET

Ana Minga's work has appeared in anthologies in Argentina, Chile, Peru, Venezuela, Mexico, Cuba, Spain, and in two Ecuadorian anthologies published in Cuenca and Quito. One of her short stories was awarded first prize in a literary competition in Villa Pedraza, Spain. Her book *A Espaldas de Dios* (which provided the entire text for this volume in English) was nominated for the biennial Hispanic-American Golden Lyric competition in Cuenca, Ecuador. Her work has appeared in many journals across the US and she was the featured poet in Autumn 2010 issue of *The Bitter Oleander*. In 2012, she was an honored guest at the Second International Conference of "A Woman's Cry" in Trujillo, Peru.

Pandemonium (Universidad Central del Ecuador, 2003)
A Espaldas de Dios (Letramía, 2006)
Pájaros Huérfanos, (Libresa, 2009)

ABOUT THE TRANSLATOR

Alexis Levitin has been translating, primarily from the Portuguese, for the last thirty-nine years. His books include Clarice Lispector's *Soulstorm* and Eugenio de Andrade's *Forbidden Words*, both published by New Directions. His most recent book is *Blood of the Sun* (Milkweed Editions, 2012) by Salgado Maranhao, a leading contemporary Brazilian poet. His translations have appeared in well over two hundred and fifty literary magazines, including *Kenyon Review, Partisan Review, Grand Street, APR,* and *Prairie Schooner.* His interest in Ecuador began six years ago and quickly resulted in the co-translation and publication of *Tapestry of the Sun: An Anthology of Ecuadorean Poetry.* Since then he has been working in collaboration with several of that country's younger poets. He is happy to see that the first to be published on her own is the courageous and provocative Ana Minga.